ISBN 0-9651034-3-9

Book design and layout: Tanya Hughes
Printed by The Stinehour Press, Lunenburg, Vermont

First Edition 9 8 7 6 5 4 3 2 1

TERRA NOVA PUBLISHING
563 Aragon St.
Pensacola, FL 32502
850.432.4540

Florida's Northwest: First Places Wild Places Favorite Places A photographic exploration of Florida's Northwest region, beginning at the Alabama state line and traveling east to the capital at Tallahassee and the 200 amazing miles in between. Stops include Perdido Key, Pensacola, Gulf Breeze, Pensacola Beach, Navarre Beach, Fort Walton Beach, Destin, DeFuniak Springs, Beaches of South Walton, Panama City, Panama City Beach, The Forgotten Coast, Marianna, Bristol, Wakulla Springs, St. Marks, and Tallahassee.

Prints from Florida's Northwest: First Places Wild Places Favorite Places are available by visiting www.emeraldcoastphotography.com.

This book is dedicated to all the stewards of Northwest Florida, those who have recognized the amazing diversity and beauty our part of the state offers to all residents and visitors. I especially would like to recognize former governor Reubin O'D. Askew and Mayor Emeritus Vince Whibbs, two men who have worked tirelessly most of their lives for the betterment of our communities and our state, inspiring me in many ways and helping ensure the outstanding quality of life for us and future generations of Northwest Florida.

FLORIDA'S NORTHWEST

FIRST PLACES
WILD PLACES
FAVORITE PLACES

Photography by Michael O'Donovan • Text by Robin Rowan

FLORIDA'S NORTHWEST

Our journey through this extraordinary region unveils a landscape of rare coastal dune lakes, miles of white sand beaches, tannin-tinted rivers, wet prairies, scrub, red bluffs and valiant last stands of old-growth pine forests. It is also one of the most biologically diverse in North America. Within a few miles of the coastline, river swamps and hammocks of red bay thrive, as do scores of endangered and threatened species–loggerhead turtles, black skimmers, carnivorous pitcher plants and sundew, and the pocket-sized Perdido and Choctawhatchee beach mice. Spotting any of these along the beach or in the woods is a rare treat as well as a gentle reminder of their fragile status.

Unprecedented growth challenges residents and politicians to step back and see what is being gained, and what may be lost. The natural beauty and miles of wide-open space that first captivated us are diminishing as more people grab their slice of paradise. The signs of "progress" throughout the region have placed us squarely at a crossroads, leaving us to ponder whether or not we're on the right path.

We offer our views of this special place to encourage exploration and an insight into why its landscapes and way of life are worth saving. Why do we so cherish an area that indulges our eccentricities, where it's *de rigeur* to mix barbeque joints with sushi bars, mullet tossing with fine arts festivals, and tarpaper shacks with gleaming high-rises? We savor the outrageous contrasts, the colorful characters, the discoveries around every bend. Woven into our vibrant tapestry are the brilliant hues of coastal dunes and windswept beaches, dense forests, bustling resorts, peaceful rural villages and centuries of a rich heritage under the flags of many nations. It is an armchair tour of a corner of the world we consider nothing short of magic.

Enjoy the ride.

Michael O'Donovan   Robin Rowan

FIRST PLACES

Surveying the emerald surf beyond sand so white you have to squint against the reflection, you dig your toes beneath the sun-warmed layer to a cooler one beneath. Before long you spot them about 50 yards offshore–seven dolphins chasing, leaping, diving, racing. To your left, a flock of pelicans in perfect "V" formation swoops inches above the water, intent on a breakfast of ladyfish…a once-in-a-lifetime moment that Northwest Floridians can experience every day. No need to wonder why we live in such a place. Verdant pine forests, wild and wacky weather, vast fields of cotton, soybeans and peanuts, winter Snowbirds and summer tourists, miles of preserved beachfront, and a rich and spirited history commingle to form the place we call Florida's Northwest. It is also the place we call home.

The scenario repeats itself countless times: Vacationers experience a week or two of our outstanding quality of life only to return home long enough to pack and call the realtor. But the joy of living here is more than pretty beaches and colorful sunsets. What fascinates us about this 200-mile stretch of trendy resort coastline, small towns and rural landscapes is its amazing diversity. It is quintessential Florida with its throngs of tourists and wide public beaches, but it blends perfectly with its Southern neighbors, Alabama and Georgia. It is far removed from the frantic toe-to-heel development of Miami and Palm Beach, but enough like that "other" Florida for residents of those overcrowded cities to look north–and to like what they see.

Mammoth military installations such as the 700-square-mile Eglin Reservation have in essence saved large portions of barrier islands and virgin pine forests from development. The federal government controls enormous amounts of land in Florida's Northwest, encompassing the islands and keys of Gulf Islands National Seashore as well as Pensacola Naval Air Station, Saufley and Corry Fields in Pensacola, Whiting Field in Milton, Eglin and Hurlburt Field in Okaloosa and Walton Counties, and Tyndall Air Force Base east of Panama City.

perpetual vacation

▲ *Pensacola loses to St. Augustine in the contest for oldest city. A Pensacola settlement attempt in 1559 failed, leaving St. Augustine to become America's oldest city, permanently established five years later.*

But the primary reason why Florida's Northwest has lagged behind the rest of the state in growth can be summed up in three words: St. Joe Company. St. Joe, called the patron saint of development by some, is also Florida's largest landowner, with holdings of 1.1 million acres, most of that in Northwest Florida. Much of the thick pine forests and coastline was purchased decades ago in anticipation of the south Florida land boom eventually reaching the north. It didn't, so St. Joe turned pines into paper.

▲ *Pensacola Naval Air Station is home base to the Blue Angels, the Navy's popular flight demonstration squadron. These retired A–4 Skyhawks are displayed in the Blue Angels Atrium at the National Museum of Naval Aviation.*

▲ *Indians, insects and isolation confronted soldiers at military outposts.*

Up until the 1990s, St. Joe was the St. Joe Paper Company, with seemingly limitless timber resources for its pulp and paper operation in Port St. Joe, Florida. But the tectonic plates of manufacturing and real estate development collided. Perhaps it was the international acclaim of "New Urbanist" architectural gems like Seaside in Walton County that started St. Joe down the path of the wildly popular walk-to-any-where neighborhood communities. Or perhaps the company realized that in an age of green building and land conservation St. Joe's polluting industry just didn't fit. Whatever it was, St. Joe dumped the paper company, hired some brilliant visionaries, and got to work designing cutting-edge communities like WaterColor, WindMark and SouthWood. If St. Joe was once Northwest Florida's anchor chain, it is now the flagship leading the development flotilla.

That same tug-of-war between preservation and economic development is happening statewide and we all look to strike the balance that is right for us. Proponents of "no growth" are doomed to be left behind as the region prepares for a massive surge in population. The secret is out, and you can't blame folks for wanting to share this remarkable place with us. While we make room for them in the form of roads, schools and hospitals, it is every bit as vital that we set aside enough green space, enough forest and coastline to preserve that atmosphere of delicious, perpetual vacation.

◄ *Turpentine workers around the turn of the 20th century would make "V"-shaped cuts in the trunk of a pine, allowing the sap to flow out into a cup. These "cat-faced" trees are scattered throughout the piney woods, some with the cups still attached!*

Florida's Northwest hasn't received nearly the amount of press given to other parts of the state; it is relegated to two pages in most state guidebooks and regularly cut off the map in others. But early in its history, it was popular with several native tribes: Apalachee, Pensacola, Creek, Choctaw. Those early civilizations found the climate mild, the rivers clear, the fish and game plentiful, the native figs and

persimmons sweet and tasty. Later, European nations clashed with Indians and with each other in an effort to claim the region and be the first to exploit her vast resources and hidden riches.

In the early 16th century, Spanish explorers–de Soto, Narvaez, Pineda, Miruelo and de Leon, among others–had extended the Spanish empire to include all of "La Florida," which at one time stretched as far west as the Mississippi River and as far north as Virginia. To strengthen that foothold, Spain would have to endure Native American uprisings, epidemics and skirmishes with French and English soldiers. The earliest Spanish settlement attempt in 1526 along coastal South Carolina was passed over by the history books, so many believe Don Tristan de Luna y Arellano's expedition in 1559 documents the first European colonization in the New World. Luna brought 1500 colonists and soldiers to Pensacola's shores, landing the fleet near "red bluffs." But just four days after the two-month voyage, the new settlers were beset by a ferocious hurricane that sank most of the fleet while at anchor, some with cattle and cargo still aboard. Dazed and disheartened survivors wandered inland to Alabama, and the settlement was finally abandoned a year and a half later.

Decades passed before Europeans returned to Florida's northern gulf coast. Spanish missions and forts were tentative signs that Spain intended to stay. However, French and English invasions temporarily thwarted those plans, and for many years control of the region shifted so frequently that troops would

This effigy from the Weedon Island culture dates back 1200 years and is said to be the finest Native American pottery artifact in the Southeast. It was discovered in the vicinity of downtown Fort Walton Beach in the 1960s.

have to check each morning to see which flag flew over a fort to know where they were sleeping that night!

Permanent possession of West Florida brought an end to the empire building when troops under General Andrew Jackson stormed Pensacola in 1814 and 1819, transferring ownership of the West Florida territory to the U.S. in 1821. It wasn't until 1845 that Florida officially became a state, and with it, a new capital at Tallahassee, halfway between the two former centers of government in Pensacola and St. Augustine.

▲ *Apache medicine man Geronimo, incarcerated at Fort Pickens on Santa Rosa Island, 1886-87*

▲ *Shells were commonly used as currency among Native Americans, and later with Europeans. To pay someone now means to "shell out" [money].*

Around the mid-19th century, other coastal areas of Florida's Northwest were beginning to thrive; specifically Apalachicola and what is now Destin. Up until this time, Florida's interior remained relatively unexplored. Especially in the low-lying peninsula, alligators, insects and disease were all that awaited anyone foolish enough to travel too far inland.

pompano,

A young fisherman from New London, Connecticut may have heard all of the seafaring tales of this remote area on the Gulf of Mexico, and became the first white man to settle on the East Pass peninsula. His name was Leonard Destin. Destin built fishing seines, or "pull boats" manned by long oars, and lived off the gulf's bounty: Pompano, sheepshead, red snapper, skipjack, and Spanish and king mackerel. He recruited other young men to the area and taught them both his seine building and fishing techniques. At its peak, 18 fish camps operated around East Pass.

sheepshead,

The trading post of Panton, Leslie and Company established at St. Marks became the most prominent trading partner with the local tribes, supplying them with goods needed for the rugged frontier life of early Florida– muskets, knives, needles and axes–in exchange for furs. When the fur trade declined, the tribes paid for goods with land. One of those parcels along the Apalachicola River was sold to the Apalachicola Land Company. Soon after, the river became a major highway for commerce and a booming port trade began in earnest. Cotton was shipped down the river from Alabama and Georgia, then to ports all over the world.

Seining uses a net with weights on the bottom and buoys on the top in areas where there are large schools of fish. The weights and floats make the net stand up in the water to encircle and trap the fish. A few of the wooden drying racks used for the enormous seine nets can still be seen around the Destin area.

Business was so good here, in fact, that land speculators attempted to settle a rival town with another port on St. Joseph Bay. They would call the town St. Joseph. By the early 1830s, St. Joseph was one of the largest towns in Florida with its port and steam-powered railroad. A bitter feud between Apalachicola and St. Joseph ensued, with the citizens of Apalachicola jokingly offering $30,000 to buy the town. They needn't have bothered, because little St. Joseph was hit with two hurricanes and a yellow fever epidemic that quickly caused the town's demise. The import of cotton was completely halted by a Union blockade during the Civil War, but the town of Apalachicola, built around the port, remained.

red snapper, skipjack

From the start of the war, Confederate troops were badly outnumbered in Pensacola. By 1862, most residents had abandoned the town. A Confederate "scorched earth" policy meant that anything the Union might perceive as valuable was removed or burned–warehouses, sawmills, wharves, lumberyards and railroads.

▼ *Off the town of Apalachicola, the river and bay merge to form one of the most pristine waterways in Florida.*

With the war over, beleaguered residents slowly returned to the region to begin the process of rebuilding. In 1866, the first shipments of Northwest Florida's most abundant resource, yellow pine, were exported to England. Ships from Europe and the far-flung reaches of the

United States loaded up on "yellow gold" as well as Apalachicola cypress. The entire region bustled, with whites and blacks working side by side in the shipyards, lumber mills, and pine forests. The Louisville & Nashville railroad through the region in 1883 opened up new land for development, and northern land companies began advertising lots in an area where the air was "healthful" and orange trees laden with ripe fruit. Idealistic hawkers of Florida's Northwest failed, however, to mention the malicious yellow fever epidemics that decimated coastal cities.

Lumber, railroads and another plentiful resource–red snapper–dominated port trade for decades, amassing enormous wealth for many families. In Pensacola, a mass exodus of these newly minted Rockefellers was taking place. Families left behind the insect and

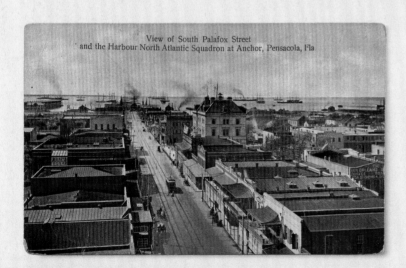

View of South Palafox Street and the Harbour North Atlantic Squadron at Anchor, Pensacola, Fla

smokestack infested waterfront (now the Seville District) to build glorious estate homes in North Hill, about a mile north of downtown. In Tallahassee, major expansion of both the state government and the Capitol building reflected the optimism of a growing region.

Wharves and tall ships once dominated the waterfront in Pensacola, which ended at Main Street. Sixty acres of land south of Main Street were created using ships' ballast from around the world–broken tile from France, red granite from Sweden, blue stones from Italy, and dredging material from the River Thames.

A local fisherman with his catch, 1906

A large contingent of Vietnamese relocated to Pensacola after 1975, fleeing the country as Saigon fell to the North, marking the end of the Vietnam War. Many men and women work as captains and crew of the Joe Patti fleet, wearing the traditional conical hats, long pants and split tunics.

Meanwhile, the building of the Panama Canal brought new excitement to the port cities of Apalachicola, Pensacola and what is now Panama City. The town of Harrison on St. Andrews Bay was changed to Panama City in 1906 to promote its port and proximity to the Panama Canal. The entire Panama City area, which had been part of both Washington and Calhoun Counties, split off to form Bay County in 1913, with Panama City as its new county seat. Even the long-abandoned town of St. Joseph on St. Joseph Bay saw a resurrection. In 1910, the name was changed to Port St. Joe, and soon after John Bennett Stone bought the entire town for about $125 in back taxes.

Panama City, Florida from the Air

A landmark court decision made in Panama City in 1963 gave every person the right to be represented in court by an attorney.

Some saw the unchecked clear-cutting of virgin pine forests and overfishing of snapper as a sign that the boom could not last, and indeed by about 1930, the entire region had bottomed out. No more lumber meant that the tall ships stopped coming. When the snapper was fished out, hundreds of commercial fishing vessels left the area, sending Northwest Florida into a slow and steady decline that would last for decades.

In 1927, about the same time as Northwest Florida was slipping into decay and poverty, south Florida was experiencing a land boom.

Local officials there were giving away prime property on Miami Beach to anyone who would build on it. The word of the boom spread

to all parts of the nation, and a young man from Delaware named Alfred duPont thought he'd do one better. He'd send his brother-in-law,

Edward Ball, to the other end of the state to purchase some land on speculation; surely the boom would eventually encompass the

entire state.

quintessential Florida

Ball returned from his first trip to report that he'd purchased 96,000 acres in Northwest Florida at just under $8 an acre. He told stories of the strange tangles of scrub so thick as to be impenetrable, people living in rural areas devastated by crushing poverty, and the most beautiful beaches he'd ever laid eyes on with absolutely no way to get to them. DuPont realized that if Northwest Florida was ever to be developed, good roads were a priority, so while Ball continued to

make additional visits to the region to purchase ever increasing amounts of land, duPont did his part in helping establish the Gulf Coast

Highway Association, through which two major east-west thoroughfares were built, Highway 90 and Highway 98. Prior to those two

highways, the main transportation route was by rail for freight, and the steamer *Tarpon* brought much-needed supplies to residents from

Pensacola to Panama City.

In one 1933 trip, Ball purchased 240,000 acres in Gulf, Bay, Liberty and Franklin Counties. The Florida land boom was a bust and the country was sinking into the Depression years. Ball was one of the few buying land. With this latest purchase, he bought the town of Port St. Joe, plus a sawmill, a railroad, a land development company, a telephone company and Port St. Joe Dock & Terminal Company. DuPont must have had his doubts about this land deal, and about Ball, since none of these companies, or the town, were an especially good bargain. With the virgin pine forests gone, both the sawmill and railroad sat idle. The few who stayed in Port St. Joe relied mostly on fishing for their living. The docks and wharves were rotting, and there was no evidence that St. Joseph, as it was once known, had been one of the most prosperous cities in the South a century earlier.

With so much pineland, duPont envisioned a paper mill at Port St. Joe, which would bring the town and the surrounding area prosperity. But duPont died before he could see his vision realized, having never set foot in Northwest Florida. At the time of his death in 1935, he owned 280,000 acres in the region, which at one time had ballooned to nearly 470,000 acres. About 200,000 of those were sold to the government to establish the Apalachicola National Forest.

Because we don't think about future generations, they will never forget us.   – *Henrik Tikkanen*

Brick Highway

When Edward Ball set off on his first junket to Northwest Florida from Jacksonville, he discovered that the paved road ended in Lake City—and didn't pick up again until just outside of Milton—a distance of some 300 miles! In between was a dirt trail mostly unimproved since the Spanish and Indian Wars a hundred years before. Imagine his delight when he came upon this beautiful stretch of highway! Three sections of the 1921 brick highway still exist and parallel Hwy. 90 between Marquis Bayou and Harold in Santa Rosa County.

▲ *The Village of Baytowne Wharf,*
Sandestin Resort, South Walton County

The paving of Highway 98 brought the promise of more travel, new people, and a fledgling tourist industry. In the early 1930s, a new concrete bridge crossed Pensacola Bay for the first time, and a bridge across the Destin Pass connected the tiny village to the outside world. Captain William Marler had been taking folks in Destin deep-sea fishing informally for a number of years when Coleman Kelly and his wife Mattie moved into the area. By 1937, the Kellys built one of the first commercial ventures at the foot of the bridge: a combination gas station, grocery and general store, restaurant and saloon plus a few small cottages for out-of-town visitors. But the real breakthrough in Destin was Coleman's *Martha-Gene*, licensed for sportfishing. Sometimes he would sleep at the store's front counter waiting for the first gas customer of the day, and usually ended up talking the driver and any passengers into a deep-sea adventure!

World War II brought an influx of pilots to Naval Air Station Pensacola and broadened the scope of all military branches throughout Florida's Northwest. In fact, every American Naval pilot trained there, as well as some British and French pilots. The demand for pilots was so great that the training period was shortened from 14 to just 7 months!

After the war, Pensacola enticed the Navy pilots and their families to vacation on its beautiful beaches. In 1960, the now-famous Pensacola Beach neon billfish sign was created, spending two years downtown prior to a move to its permanent Gulf Breeze location.

Ed and Dorothy Coffeen owned a fish camp in Walton County that spanned from Four Mile Point on Choctawhatchee Bay (now part of Sandestin Resort) to the Gulf of Mexico (now Four Mile Village). During World War II, they leased the land to the Army at Eglin Field for $1 a year. The Army built roads, 22 buildings, and a ramp up the side of a sand dune to test the American version of the German V-1 rocket. After the war, the Coffeens turned the mess hall into their home, and Dorothy Coffeen deeded a large portion of the land to the Sierra Club to establish the Coffeen Nature Preserve.

In the next few decades, Florida's Northwest mirrored the direction of cities in many other parts of America—decaying downtowns watched residents flee to the suburbs and malls replaced downtown shopping. As desegregation was forced on the South, clashes between races were inevitable. Several Pensacola families filed the state's first class-action integration lawsuit to send their children to previously all-white schools. There were demonstrations to integrate lunch counters, but real progress was slow. As late as 1976, race-driven riots against integration at Escambia High School made national headlines. But there were reasons for optimism, too. Tourism, charter fishing, new universities and junior colleges and military installations buoyed the region. By the 1990s, Northwest Florida would see its most

profound changes yet as a company most knew only by its ownership of a paper mill made inroads into development like a tornado through a trailer park.

With the hiring in 1997 of CEO Peter Rummell came a new era for the St. Joe Company, as it is now called. The transition from paper to real estate development positioned St. Joe in the global marketplace, and the change in the entire region would be dramatic and permanent. "Place-making" was Rummell's new mantra, and St. Joe made itself over almost overnight. That same year, St. Joe purchased real estate giant Arvida, then Prudential Florida Realty, creating a development empire and strategically setting its sights on Florida's Northwest.

To offset the public perception that St. Joe might develop its entire acreage in Northwest Florida, the company began selling huge tracts of environmentally sensitive parcels to the State of Florida in Bay, Franklin, Walton, Wakulla, Gulf and Liberty Counties. In its first planned developments, Rummell talked about "clustering" of neighborhoods, leaving large green spaces in between. The original concept for Seaside, Florida, the acclaimed catalyst for the "New Urbanism," was expanded, with an emphasis on dune preservation, native species and architectural appeal. And to show its commitment to the counties as well as provide access to its developments, St. Joe was giving away as much land as it was developing–land to widen Highway 98, the major east-west thoroughfare; land for a new high school in Bay County, a new medical complex in Walton County, and a controversial new airport.

Besides the sparsely developed Gulf County where the former paper mill is located, St. Joe owns the most land–191,000 acres–in adjoining Bay County (Panama City, Panama City Beach), enough land to change the face of the entire area.

opportunities

Throughout Florida's Northwest, hundreds of other developers are adding their signatures to the remaking of the region. Several hurricanes have also provided communities with opportunities to shape growth as they rebuild. "Visioning" meetings in Bay, Okaloosa, Santa Rosa and Escambia Counties have allowed residents to help decide the future direction of their communities.

to shape

St. Joe plans to sell hundreds of thousands of inland acres that it deems "undevelopable for 15 or 20 years." Even with that amount of land out of the mix, the acreage it plans to eventually develop is staggering. Because the company kept its pinelands nearly intact for decades, this part of the state came to be known as "Florida's Last Frontier." The new St. Joe may be a kinder, gentler, more environmentally sensitive company since the days of Ed Ball, but because it controls so much land, citizens must become the watchdogs of responsible development. And along with it, ensure the preservation of enough wild beauty and open space for future generations to enjoy. Isn't that what brought us here in the first place?

growth

wild places

It is a never-ending delight to cross bridges or navigate bay, bayou and sound to barrier islands, where time moves to the rhythm of tides and waves. As you face the Gulf of Mexico, listening only to the constant movement of water, the rustle of sea oats atop the blinding whiteness of ancient dunes and the occasional cry of a gull, there is no overdevelopment, no traffic snarls, no deadlines. Just you and the sparkling, eternal waters, a scene that entices a thousand people a day to move to Florida.

In more than 1300 miles of Florida gulf and oceanfront, beaches in Florida's Northwest continue to rank in the top ten nationwide for sheer scenic beauty, public access and preserved acreage.

While we sing the praises of our beaches, there is much more to Florida's Northwest than her coastline; in some places, 70 miles separates the coast from the Georgia border. Within, tall red bluffs, underground caverns, hammocks of red oak, cypress domes, old-growth pine flatwoods, marshes, bogs, cool, clear rivers and soggy lowlands create unique ecosystems, where some of the state's most rare and endangered plants, birds, reptiles and mammals make their home.

We revisit these wild places to discover new delights: A fresh bear track along a sandy trail. Shiny black skimmers nesting on a remote beach. A profusion of blue lupine hugging the shore of a coastal lake. It may be one of the last places in Florida where a two-day hike can get you precisely to the middle of nowhere. In a world of asphalt, noise and lives dictated by the clock, these wonders of the natural world are a one-way ticket from the stresses of civilization, making it all the more vital to ensure that they remain.

Nature's magnificence unfolds.

Cypress
"knees"
provide a
sunning spot
for a resting
reptile

The natural evolution of land and sea leaves patterns and shapes in sand and shore, and occasionally, intricately carved driftwood.

This weathered, wind-swept magnolia has survived an estimated 500 years atop the "Sugar Bowl" dune preserve on Pensacola Beach. The series of photos was taken over a 15-year time period.

For a coastal area surrounded by water in its gulf, bays, bayous and rivers, nature's force and fury continues to reshape and redefine the landscape. Great inflows of water carved out bluffs, caverns and sinkholes. Severe winter storms pushed water onshore and trapped it there, forming brackish coastal lakes. Hurricanes create new passes through islands, erode shorelines and add real estate to areas that were once underwater. Extreme winds and tidal surge can devastate a city, the way 2004's Hurricane Ivan thrashed Pensacola. But barrier islands lived up to their name in a spate of hurricanes over the last decade, taking the initial impact of storms to protect the mainland. Building seaward of primary dune lines, or worse, replacing primary dunes with high-rises, is perhaps one practice where we have at last learned our lesson.

regenerate

As with any coastal landscape, the shoreline is continually moving, shifting, changing. Prior to the last Ice Age the Florida coastline was 30 miles seaward, and the land we know as Florida many times larger than it is today. The evolution continues despite our Herculean efforts to stop it.

Water…for boating, for swimming, fishing, drinking, for *life*…we take for granted that it will always be plentiful, accessible, and clean. Our seafood industry and the thousands of fishermen and support workers whose livelihoods depend on it fight for increased treatment for stormwater, against offshore drilling, and, in short, for their survival. What they want, and what all of us want, are clear, unpolluted waterways for fishing and recreation and an abundance of fresh, untainted seafood. A fast-growing population coupled with poor growth planning can have a startling impact on our waterways. As an example, oyster beds need clean water to grow. Ninety-eight percent of the Apalachicola River system is open to oystering, while only 1 to 2 percent of the densely populated area

and renew

Aerial view of Big Sabine Bay

around the Pensacola Bay system is open. Industrial pollutants have also infiltrated the Floridan aquifer in Pensacola, the area's sole source of drinking water, while thousands of pounds of groundwater toxins flow unchecked into area waterways. The region's population could double in the next twenty years, making clean water issues more vital than ever. Man's impact on the land is more terrible and more formidable than any force of nature. He is the only creature on Earth to knowingly poison his own environment, but also possesses the will and determination to restore it.

This Pensacola Beach resident maintains his sense of humor even after Hurricane Ivan ravaged his home.

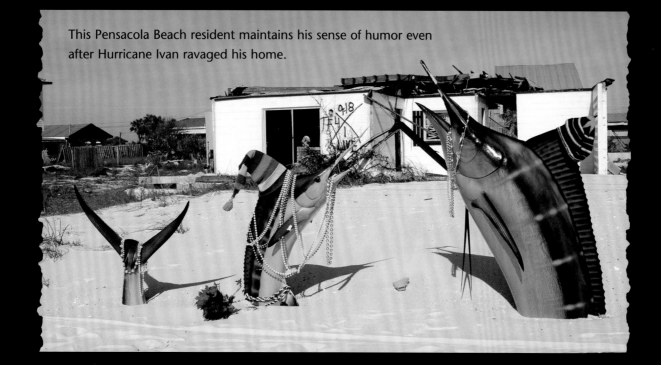

Aside from the destructive forces of wind and water, they are always with us, and like fire, serve to continually regenerate and renew.

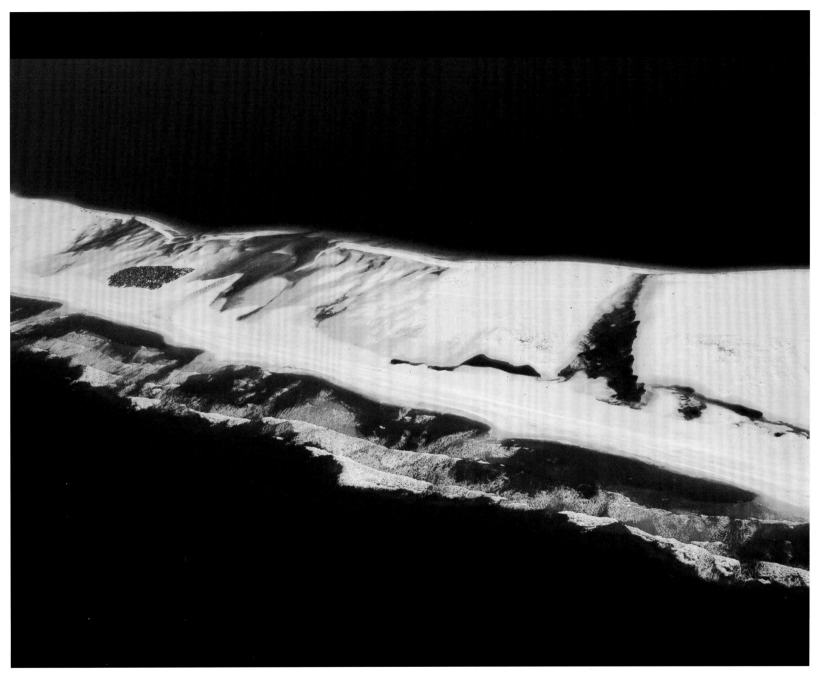

This island washover, compliments of Hurricane Ivan, carries the sand and dunes from the gulf side of the islands and spreads them across a wide area on the sound side, creating large "fans," or sand flats.

Fall foliage in Florida's Northwest.

▲ Black Bear, Sugar Bowl dune, Pensacola Beach

▲ Giant sea turtles leave the gulf to nest near the dunes

▲ Raccoons can open oysters with their sharp claws

▲ Red foxes are making a comeback in Florida's Northwest

This net
fisherman
displays
perfect form

▲ Female blue crabs "paint their fingernails" (have red-tipped claws). Male claws are all blue.

Thousands of butterflies stop in Florida's Northwest on their way to Mexico each fall. How they can travel up to 50 miles a day and over open gulf waters in wind, waves and storms remains a mystery.

Wiregrass

White-topped pitcher plant

Coastal dune lake

Green areas denote the more than one million acres of The Gulf Coastal Plain Ecosystem Partnership (GCPEP).

Longleaf Pine seedling

One of the most ambitious conservation projects in the state to date reconnects more than a million acres of old-growth longleaf pine ecosystem from Gulf Islands National Seashore north to the Conecuh National Forest in Alabama. **The Gulf Coastal Plain Ecosystem Partnership (GCPEP)** is a collaborative effort on behalf of several public and private landowners including the Department of Defense, The Nature Conservancy, the Florida Department of Environmental Protection and International Paper. The unlikely partners are joining forces to protect and manage the "exceptional" biodiversity of this area.

▲ The shallows along the Intracoastal Waterway are perfect for fly-fishing

▲ Hwy. 98 hugs the shoreline of St. Joseph Bay

▲ Lake Wimico near Port St. Joe meets the Intracoastal Waterway

▲ The canals at Range Point

Perdido River, Escambia County

Float lazily down one of Northwest Florida's tranquil and shallow freshwater rivers such as the Coldwater or Sweetwater, or gear up for a more ambitious canoeing or kayaking adventure on the Perdido, Yellow, or Blackwater.

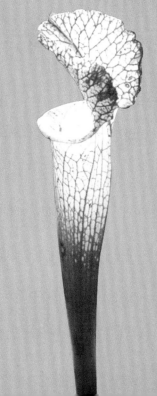

▲ St. George Island State Park

Pensacola-St. Augustine Road (Old Spanish Trail), inside Naval Live Oaks Reserve, Gulf Islands National Seashore

Off the trail at Fort Pickens, Gulf Islands National Seashore

Nature trail
at Bay Bluffs
Park along
Scenic Highway,
Pensacola

Only the big dogs make it in the Florida scrub. A scrub environment is characterized by small, gnarled trees, shrubs and perennials like prickly-pear cactus. Without the shade of trees, it is hotter and drier than other Florida landscapes. Blowing sand will bury many small plants, and regular fires caused by lightning strikes determine which plants will prevail. Sand pine, Florida rosemary, and saw palmetto do well in this harsh beach environment.

Topsail Hill State Preserve near Sandestin Resort has been called the most pristine piece of land in Florida, virtually unchanged since Spanish conquistadors tromped ashore five centuries ago.

▲ Quittin' time...

Steps from the sky-scraping high-rises of Panama City Beach is a world far removed from the frenzied tourist lifestyle. A keen eye, quiet, and a little patience will yield a payoff of whitetail deer, alligators or white ibis at St. Andrews State Recreation Area off Thomas Drive. Bottle-nosed dolphin are also known to follow the excursion boats to Shell Island.

▲ Cruising the Intracoastal Waterway

Before motors or steam, the wind was the only way to power a ship through the wilds of our waterways. In the late 1800s it wasn't unusual to see a hundred or more "tall ships" in Pensacola Bay.

WHY SHOULD WE SAVE ENDANGERED SPECIES?

Why is it important to save the red-cockaded woodpecker, the Florida rosemary bush, the

Florida bog frog or any endangered or threatened species?

•   Less than 1% of all plant species worldwide have been screened for their possible medicinal uses, while we lose up to

     100 species daily. More than one-third of the most commonly prescribed drugs come from extracts found in plants

     and animals. For example, a common plant here in Northwest Florida is the prickly pear. Nearly every part of this

     cactus has been used to treat ailments from diarrhea and asthma to ulcers and tumors. Plus the juice from its plump

     red fruit makes a terrific cake, and cooking the cactus pads is a healthy alternative to green beans -

     but watch out for those spikes!

•   Thirty thousand species of edible plants have been identified throughout the world, but humans depend on 20

     species (corn, rice, soybeans) to provide 90% of the world's food.

•   A diversity of plant and animal species signals a healthy ecosystem, something we depend on to purify the air, clean

     our water and supply our food. When a species becomes endangered, it throws the balance off, which can affect an

     entire ecosystem.

•   Think about where you go to hike, bike, camp, fish or swim. Eco-tourism is a multi-billion-dollar industry, and people

     like to travel to places like Northwest Florida where they can see species that exist nowhere else in the world. The

     annual Monarch migration, scalloping, crabbing, charter fishing and a thousand other outdoor activities are all

     dependent upon a healthy environment.

The brilliant
blooms of a
trumpet vine
frame a time-
worn window in
Apalachicola.

▲　Stop for alligator jerky, air plants and shell nightlights at the numerous roadside souvenir shops.

Despite galloping development of linear subdivisions, outlet malls and chain restaurants, Florida's Northwest retains a hefty dose of character, charm, and yes, kitsch. Right beside the fancy resort condos and golf course villas, visitors flock to play a round of Goofy Golf or attend the annual mullet toss. Locals proudly point to the flashy, trashy Pensacola Beach neon fish sign as one of their favorite landmarks. And who wouldn't want to remember their vacation by having their photo taken with "Big Gus," the giant steer in front of Angelo's Steak House in Panama City? Those outdated "space age" motel signs, rejuvenated historic districts and classy waterfront developments give our towns and beaches their unique flavor. By contrast, travel the country to see endless homogenized landscapes of fast-food shops and chain motels, devoid of a sense of place, and labeled "Generica" by gurus of responsible growth.

Walton County once trumpeted the fact that its entire southern half had no fast-food restaurants, honky-tonk bars or T-shirt shops. Now the Whataburgers and Tom Thumbs have infiltrated even the highest of the highbrow areas. Conversely, Panama City Beach recently bulldozed its main core of tacky

FAVORITE PLACES

Spring Break beach hotels (and with it Miracle Strip Amusement Park, a 1963 landmark) in an attempt to appeal to more monied visitors. The allure of the 1950s architecture, albeit a bit run-down, was that the white sand welcome mat was rolled out to anyone. The playful signs with dolphins and seashells beckoned to visitors that this was a place to come and have fun, to kick back and have a great time if you were from New York City or Dothan, Alabama. And on Pensacola Beach, tiny cinderblock homes that parlayed its laid-back atmosphere were mostly destroyed after two crushing hurricanes, only to be replaced by a series of fenced-off McMansions that scream "Keep Out!"

We're certainly not against newcomers or their considerable influence. They're part of the reason we are lucky enough to have symphonies, ballet companies, and world-class art galleries and museums. And that, in turn, attracts military retirees and other highly educated people here to fill high-tech sector jobs. But we also cherish the generations of families who work the way their fathers and grandfathers did before them—net fishing, oystering, farming, shrimping. It is exactly that Yin and Yang, those opposing but complementing forces that supply the region's enduring heart and soul.

To this roux we begin adding landscapes, quirky attractions, ordinary and fascinating people, a bit of lore, history, and a mix of cultures and ethnicities to the pot, cooking up a spicy gumbo that is our little corner of Florida. Dish yourself up a hefty bowlful as you try a taste of some of our favorite spots.

Grayton Beach

With local favorites
Patrone's and the
Grayton Café
replaced by
higher-end shops
and eateries, Grayton
Beach might be a
little less laid-back
but it's just as much
fun. Get off the main
road and wander
its narrow, shady
avenues. Expect
people to wave.
And no, they don't
know you. It's
the South, y'all.

The Red Bar
delivers an unusual mix of patrons: Tennis ladies, aging hippies and pierced and tattooed Gen-Xers all enjoy the eclectic atmosphere.

Grayton Beach State Park

▲ Kayakers on Western Lake, one of 13 coastal dune lakes in Florida's Northwest.

▲ Seaside

Rising out of the Florida scrub, the little town of Seaside on 30-A in South Walton County was the first of the "walk-to-anywhere" neighborhood communities, and the model for what is now known as "The New Urbanism." Robert Davis's vision has become a victim of its own success, spawning dozens of new towns across America, among them Rosemary Beach and WaterColor, both along 30-A.

▲ Rosemary Beach

▼ Seaside

▼ WaterSound, along 30-A

▼ WaterColor, a St. Joe Co. development between Grayton Beach and Seaside

A cloud "pours" from an umbrella rim like a genie from a bottle.

▲ More than 80 percent of the land encompassing **Gulf Islands National Seashore** is underwater, but its barrier islands and keys are its most outstanding feature, stretching 160 miles from Cat Island off coastal Mississippi east to Okaloosa Island between Destin and Fort Walton Beach.

▲ Marc Schormann, boat builder

▲ Perdido Key workout

▲ Gibson Inn, Apalachicola

Apalachicola

The "Appalach," as the locals call themselves, trace their lineage to a string of innovators and adapters. Dr. Alvin Wentworth Chapman became the South's leading botanist in the early 19th century. Marc Schormann (pictured above), an engineer and boat builder, relocated from Estonia in the 1990s to build a 28-foot steam-powered boat from the ground up. But Dr. John Gorrie topped them all. He made Florida possible for millions of residents. While living in Apalachicola, Dr. Gorrie pioneered the manufacture of ice, refrigeration and air-conditioning, receiving the first patent in 1851. His invention was driven by a need to cool the rooms of his malaria patients. At least for Floridians, the invention of air-conditioning would put Gorrie on a par with Bell, Marconi, Newton and Einstein!

Indian Pass Trading Post, along the Forgotten Coast

The first "trading post" built in 1903 on this spot was actually a commissary for the local "stillers" who turned pine tree sap into resin and turpentine. The current building dates to 1929. And in case you were wondering, a "raw bar" has nothing whatsoever to do with sushi. It means oysters, and plenty of them--shucked, plucked and sucked, the way nature intended--RAW right off the shell or on a cracker with just a little drip of hot sauce.

World's smallest police station, Carrabelle ▷

▼ Shrimp boat along the Intracoastal Waterway

Apalachicola once was a thriving city with a bustling cotton port. After the Civil War, the little town on the magnificent bay and river turned to fishing and oystering. Oystermen and women are sometimes called "tongers" for the huge homemade rakes they use to grab the oysters from the bay bottom. Each has an extensive knowledge of and a deep respect for the clean, clear water that provides their livelihood.

▲ Bookstore, Apalachicola

▲ Browsing one of the quaint shops in downtown Apalachicola

"Never doubt that
a small group of
thoughtful, committed
citizens can change
the world; indeed,
it is the only thing
that ever has."

- Margaret Mead
(1901-1978)

Destin

Rivaled only perhaps by the Florida Keys is this panorama of water colors at Destin Pass. Deep emerald, aquamarine, turquoise, violet and indigo ribbons of color dance in the dappled sunlight, flirting with the dozens of boats docked in the shallows on warm weekends.

St. Marks

Lighthouse Road at
**St. Marks National
Wildlife Refuge**
rewards visitors not only
with this magnificent
vista at the end of the
7-mile drive, but with all
manner of wildlife sight-
ings. Listen for the lilting
song of a wood thrush,
or stop to get an up-close
look at the profusion
of St. John's wort,
the carnivorous red
sundew, or the white
flowers of the duck
potato sprouting from
a nearby canal.

▲ White-tailed deer

▼ Osprey and nest

Wakulla Springs

▶

Cruise up the Wakulla River to spot alligators, water moccasin, anhingas, limpkin, gallinules and box turtles in such profusion it's hard to imagine they're real. But believe it: The staff of the park does not interact with the wildlife in any way except perhaps to poke the nose of the occasional curious alligator that wanders into the swimming area. The setting itself is worth the trip with its moss-draped cypress centered around the world's deepest natural spring. **The Edward Ball Wakulla Springs State Park** is 14 miles south of Tallahassee on State Road 267.

▶

The Anhinga, or "snake" bird, can dive underwater for fish but must first dry its wings before flying.

"Do you know how fast you have to run if a alligator is chasin' you?" queries the tour boat captain to a group of school children on the Wakulla Springs River Cruise. After seeing their wide-eyed expressions, he breaks into a broad smile and answers "Jes' a little bit faster than the persons you's with!"

Movie producers were smitten with the primordial scenery around Wakulla Springs: Some of Johnny Weismuller's "Tarzan" movies were shot here, as well as the 1954 B-movie cult classic "Creature from the Black Lagoon."

▲ St. George Island State Park

▲ Winter on Apalachicola River

What a strange juxtaposition to have a nondescript tower rising out of the top of the grand **Old Capitol Building**, which was built in 1845, the same year Florida joined the Union. The older Capitol building is set up as a legislative museum, where you will see exhibits interpreting the state's political history, constitutions, and read that the first building to house the legislature was made of pine logs. The

Drive twelve miles out of Tallahassee on Centerville Road and stop in at **Bradley's Country Store** for some homemade sausage and a little news and gossip. Four generations of Bradleys have kept the recipes and the ambience of the little store alive since 1927.

This small marker near the Capitol Building in Tallahassee is the **prime meridian** for the state, meaning that every piece of property is mapped in relation to this point. Meridian Road in Tallahassee runs along this imaginary line.

Five roads throughout the Tallahassee area–Centerville, Miccosukee, Meridian, Old St. Augustine and Old Bainbridge–receive special protection for their giant bearded oaks. These **canopy roads** were once major trade routes for cotton and many other crops from farms and plantations in the surrounding countryside. From Tallahassee, the crops were sent south to the gulf for shipping elsewhere. Today they are a pleasant reminder of a slower, more genteel time.

Mission San Luis on West Mission Road northwest of Florida State University in Tallahassee was the western capital of "La Florida" as well as home to more than 1500 Apalachee Indians, Spanish friars, soldiers and colonists. From the mid-17th century until 1704, the settlers established some of the first ranches and farms in Florida, then traded their agricultural products with Havana. Although there were occasional uprisings, an impending raid in 1704 forced the abandonment of the mission. Recreated settlement buildings, living history and exhibits are free and open to the public.

▲ Hay rolls

▲ Old barn, Bristol

One of Franklin Roosevelt's New Deal agencies, the Civilian Conservation Corps, was responsible for beginning a Florida state park system; a team was assigned to this area near Marianna in 1935. While constructing some of the park facilities, one of the workers discovered a deep hole under the roots of a fallen tree. Upon further investigation, he came upon the wondrous formations that have become the top attraction at the **Florida Caverns State Park** off I-10 3 miles north of Marianna.

From 1885 until 1922, the "winter assembly" of the New York Chautauqua met in **DeFuniak Springs** for art, culture and history. Formal education at the time was sketchy at best, and the Chautauqua provided a means to educate and enlighten the public with lectures, demonstrations, performances and exhibits. A revival of the **Florida Chautauqua** is held each February in the Victorian town, built around a perfectly round spring-fed lake. DeFuniak Springs is off I-10 at Hwy. 331.

▲ Julee Cottage (1805), Historic Pensacola Village

▲ Entrance to a Seville Historic District garden

▲ Outdoor concerts as well as music and arts festivals fill the shady and historic Seville Square in Pensacola.

Christ Church on Seville Square in Pensacola is the oldest in Florida, built in 1832. In 1988, archaeologists discovered three early rectors buried under the church. A special ceremony reconsecrating their remains was held in the church two months later. Over the years, the church was used to house both Union and Confederate troops, an African-American Episcopal congregation, a library and a museum.

▲ **Pensacola Beach**

▲ Atop a high dune this cross commemorates the first mass in the New World, August 14, 1559.

FLORIDA
$1.00
SANDOLLARS
75¢
HONOR
SYSTEM

▲ Krewe of Wrecks Mardi Gras parade

Surfers head out to catch a wave.

RESOURCES

Florida State Parks

Alfred B. Maclay Gardens State Park
Tallahassee, FL (850) 487-4556

Bald Point State Park
Alligator Point, FL (850) 349-9146

Big Lagoon State Park
Pensacola, FL (850) 492-1595

Blackwater River State Park
Holt, FL (850) 983-5363

Camp Helen State Park
Santa Rosa Beach, FL (850) 231-4210

Constitution Convention Museum State Park
Port St. Joe, FL (850) 229-8029

Deer Lake State Park
Santa Rosa Beach, FL (850) 231-4210

Econfina River State Park
Lamont, FL (850) 922-6007

Eden Gardens State Park
Point Washington, FL (850) 231-4214

Falling Waters State Park
Chipley, FL (850) 638-6130

Florida Caverns State Park
Marianna, FL (850) 482-9598

Fred Gannon Rocky Bayou State Park
Niceville, FL (850) 833-9144

Grayton Beach State Park
Santa Rosa Beach, FL (850) 231-4210

Henderson Beach State Park
Destin, FL (850) 837-7550

John Gorrie Museum State Park
Apalachicola, FL (850) 653-9347

Lake Jackson Mounds Archaeological State Park
Tallahassee, FL (850) 922-6007

Lake Talquin State Park
Tallahassee, FL (850) 922-6007

Letchworth Mounds Archaeological State Park
Monticello, FL (850) 922-6007

Natural Bridge Battlefield Historic State Park
Tallahassee, FL (850) 922-6007

Navarre Beach State Park
Navarre, FL (850) 936-6188

Ochlockonee River State Park
Sopchoppy, FL (850) 962-2771

Ormon House
Apalachicola, FL (850) 653-1209

Perdido Key State Park
Pensacola, FL (850) 492-1595

Ponce de Leon Springs State Park
Ponce de Leon, FL (850) 836-4281

San Marcos de Apalache Historic State Park
St. Marks, FL (850) 925-6216

St. Andrews State Park
Panama City, FL (850) 233-5140

St. George Island State Park
St. George Island, FL (850) 927-2111

(T. H. Stone Memorial) St. Joseph Peninsula State Park
Port St. Joe, FL (850) 227-1327

Tarkiln Bayou Preserve State Park
Pensacola, FL (850) 492-1595

Three Rivers State Park
Sneads, FL (850) 482-9006

Topsail Hill Preserve State Park
Santa Rosa Beach, FL (850) 267-0299

Torreya State Park
Bristol, FL (850) 643-2674

(Edward Ball) Wakulla Springs State Park
Wakulla Springs, FL (850) 224-5950

National Parks and Forests

Apalachicola National Forest
Apalachicola Ranger District (west)
PO Box 579 • Bristol FL 32321
(850) 643-2282

Wakulla Ranger District (east)
1773 Crawfordville Highway
Crawfordville FL 32327 • (850) 926-3561

Gulf Islands National Seashore
Headquarters 1801 Gulf Breeze Parkway
Gulf Breeze, FL (850) 934-2600

Seashore areas:
Fort Pickens Area - western tip of Santa Rosa Island
pre-Civil War fort, hiking/biking trails, camp-
grounds, fishing pier, picnic areas

Santa Rosa Day-Use Area - Opal Beach between
Pensacola Beach and Navarre Beach - picnic
pavilions, interpretive center, beaches

Johnson Beach - Perdido Key - off State Road
292 - picnic pavilions, beaches

Fort Barrancas aboard Pensacola Naval Air Station
pre-Civil War fort, Advanced Redoubt, hiking
trails, gift shop

Naval Live Oaks Reservation - east of Gulf Breeze -
Visitor Center, hiking trails

Okaloosa Island between Destin and Fort Walton
Beach - bay beach, picnic area

Environmental Groups

Apalachicola Bay & Riverkeeper
23 Ave. D • Apalachicola, FL 32320
(850) 653-8936

Friends of Perdido Bay
10738 Lillian Hwy.
Pensacola, FL 32506
(850) 453-5488
www.friendsofperdidobay.com

Gulf Coast Environmental Defense
P.O. Box 732
Gulf Breeze, FL 32562
(850) 432-3001
www.pcola.com/gced

Gulf Coastal Plain Ecosystem Partnership
4025 Highway 178
Jay, FL 32565
(850) 675-5758

The Nature Conservancy (local office)
4025 Highway 178
Jay, FL 32565
(850) 675-5758
www.tnc.org

Pensacola Gulf Coastkeeper
811 W. Garden Street
Pensacola, FL 32501
(850) 429-8422
www.coastkeepers.org

Santa Rosa Sound Coalition
(850) 932-3077

Sierra Club - NWF Group
P.O. Box 4907
Seaside, FL 32459-4907
(850) 234-9206
www.florida.sierraclub.org/northwest/

Wakulla/Aucilla Waterkeeper
Florida Wildlife Federation
56 Red Bud Lane
Crawfordville, FL 32327
(850) 942-0990

History/Archaeology

Apalachicola Area Historical Society
P.O. Box 75 • Apalachicola, FL 32329

Archaeology Institute
University of West Florida
11000 University Parkway
Pensacola, FL 32514 (850) 474-3015
www.uwf.edu/archaeology/

Division of Historical Resources
Bureau of Historic Preservation
R.A. Gray Building, 4th Floor
500 South Bronough Street
Tallahassee, FL 32399-0350
www.floridatrust.org

Pensacola Archeological Society
P.O. Box 13251
Pensacola, FL 32591
(850) 474-3015 or (850) 474-2087

Pensacola Historical Museum
115 E. Zaragosa Street
Pensacola, FL 32501
(850) 433-1559

Pensacola Historical Society/Resource Center
110 E. Church Street
Pensacola, FL 32501
www.pensacolahistory.org
(850) 434-5455

Special Collections and West Florida Archives
University of West Florida Library
11000 University Parkway
Pensacola, FL 32514-5750
(850) 474-2213

Wakulla County Historical Society
P.O. Box 151
Crawfordville, FL 32326-0151

Tourism Agencies/Visitor Information

30-A.com Scenic Website (Beaches of South Walton)
www.30-a.com/discover/seaside.asp

Apalachicola Bay Chamber of Commerce
Chamber Office and Visitor Center
122 Commerce Street • Apalachicola, FL 32320
(850) 653-9419 • www.apalachicolabay.org

Beaches of South Walton Visitor Information
P.O. Box 1248 • Santa Rosa Beach, FL 32459
(850) 822-6877 • www.beachesofsouthwalton.com

Carrabelle Area Chamber of Commerce
105 St. James Ave. • P.O. Drawer DD
Carrabelle, FL 32322 • (850) 697-2585
www.carrabellechamber.org

Emerald Coast Convention & Visitors Bureau, Inc.
1540 Miracle Strip Parkway
Fort Walton Beach, FL 32548
(850) 651-7131; (800) 322-3319
www.destin-fwb.com

Gulf County Tourism Development Council
(850) 229-7800; (800) 482-GULF

Panama City Beaches Chamber of Commerce
415 Beckrich Road, Ste 200
Panama City Beach, FL 32407
(850) 235-1159
www.pcbeach.org

Pensacola/Destin/Panama City Beach Visitor Information
www.tripsmarter.com

Pensacola Bay Area Convention & Visitors Bureau
1401 East Gregory Street
Pensacola, FL 32502
(850) 434-1234; (800) 874-1234

Pensacola Beach Visitors Information Center
Santa Rosa Island Authority
P.O. Drawer 1208
Pensacola Beach, FL 32562
(800) 635-4803
www.visitpensacolabeach.com

Santa Rosa County Chamber of Commerce
5247 Stewart Street
Milton, FL 32570
(850) 623-2339
www.srcchamber.com

Santa Rosa County Visitor Information Center
8543 Navarre Pkwy.
Navarre, FL 32566
(850) 939-2691
www.beaches-rivers.com

Tallahassee Visitor Information Center
106 East Jefferson Street
(850) 413-9200; (800) 628-2866
www.secure.imarcsgroup.com/leoncountytdc

Washington County Chamber of Commerce
685 7th St. • Chipley, FL 32428
(850) 638-4157

www.emeraldcoastphotography.com

INDEX

www.emeraldcoastphotography.com

FLORIDA'S NORTHWEST

First Places Wild Places Favorite Places

ORDER FORM

Need additional books? Here's how to order:

By phone: 850.432.4540

By mail: **TERRA NOVA PUBLISHING**
563 Aragon Street
Pensacola, FL 32502

$29.95

[Plus $3.95 shipping]

Please fill out the form below and include it with your order.

Name _____

Address _____

City _____ State _____ ZIP _____

Number of copies: _____ x $29.95 ea., plus $3.95 shipping [$33.90] = _____

[Florida residents please add 7.5% sales tax]

Order total $ _____

[Make checks payable to Terra Nova Publishing]

Please allow 2-3 weeks for delivery.

Your favorite photos from this book are available at www.emeraldcoastphotography.com